DEFENSE OF THE
ORTHODOX CATHOLIC DOCTRINES OF THE LATINS

John Bessarion,
Cardinal-Archbishop of Nicaea

Translated by: D.P. Curtin

Dalcassian
Publishing
Company

PHILADELPHIA, PA

DEFENSE OF THE ORTHODOX CATHOLIC DOCTRINES

Copyright @ 2009 Dalcassian Publishing Company

All rights reserved. No part of this publication may be reproduced, distributed, or transmitted in any form or by any means, including photocopying, recording, or other electronic or mechanical methods, without the prior written permission of the publisher, except in the case of brief quotations embodied in critical reviews and certain other non-commercial uses permitted by copyright law. For permission request, write to Dalcassian Publishing Company at dalcassianpublishing at gmail.com

ISBN: 979-8-8691-6893-1 (Paperback)

Library of Congress Control Number:
Author: Curtin, D.P. (1985-)

Printed by Ingram Content Group, 1 Ingram Blvd, La Vergne, Tennessee

First printing edition 2009.

DEFENSE OF THE ORTHODOX CATHOLIC DOCTRINES

BESSARION'S DEFENSES OF THE CORRECT CATHOLIC DOGMA OF THE LATIN
CONCERNING THE PROCESSION OF THE HOLY SPIRIT AGAINST THE GREEK AND LATIN HERETICS WHICH ARE AGAINST HIM

After the council of Lyons, at the time of Gregory X, declaring his intention, and the uncelebrated authority, in which the Greek orators were united to the Roman churches, they professed that the Holy Spirit proceeds from the Father and the Son, as the Catholic Church believes and professes. Now, a certain Patriarch of Constantinople named Vecchus, adhering to the truth in the attack of his adversaries, of whom there was still a great number, turned over with great diligence the volumes of all the Greek teachers, and gathered together all their authorities on this subject, and by some titles presided over by him, as it seemed necessary from the continual contention which then took place, as if the Holy Spirit is from the Father and the Son. That from the Father through the Son, that directly from the Father, and so on of the like. To each of these titles he adapted the various authorities of different teachers; proving by them what was proposed to him, for example, in the first chapter he cites the authorities by which it is proved that the Holy Spirit is also from the Son. At other times proving that it is from the Father through the Son. Finally, to show that it is the same thing to say from the Father and the Son, and from the Father through the Son, so that we may be instructed, when we hear the Greek teachers theologizing the Holy Spirit from the Father through the Son, that we should understand the same thing, as if we heard them say that from the Father and the Son. He cites other authorities signifying the equivalence of these prepositions in theology. And to this title, and to all the others, he put forward a certain argument, concluding his intelligence in the best way that was intended for him. Some years after the aforesaid Vecchus, a certain one among the Greeks named Gregory, surnamed Palamas, of whom the Greeks had great esteem, was contrary to the Catholic truth concerning this article, and was an open enemy, wishing to weaken all the labors of the aforesaid Vecchus by a few, contradicted his arguments and prologues, wishing to prove the authorities proposed, not what he said, but to have a very different intention. If this had been true, all the work of the aforesaid patriarch would have disappeared. And yet men persisted in this opinion for many years. But when this work of both came into the hands of myself, Bessarius, cardinal-bishop of Tusculana, then archbishop of Nicae. I did not suffer it, nor did I take it with an equal mind, that even the common teachers should suffer the slander, and for the convicted and diligent falsehood of some this most wise man, Vecchus, the patriarch. Wherefore I set myself against Palamas and his murky and apparent contradictions, proving that the authorities produced have that intention which Vecchus most wisely says; not as Palamas slanderously explains. On this presupposition, all the authorities do their best for the intended purpose, and the truth appears in all things more clearly to those who look. Therefore, first the arguments or prologues of Vecchus are presented, then Palamas's contradictions to them, and finally our defenses, with which we open the taunts of Palamas defending Vecchus, and set them aside as possible, if the judgment of others is correct and sufficient.

I have raised the first argument.
He collects the various authorities of different teachers, by which it is proved that the Holy Spirit is also from the Son. Others are also added after them in this volume to show that the Holy Spirit is through the Son from the Father. And when those from the Son demonstrate that they are the same Spirit through the Son, in order to prove the equivalence of these prepositions.

Clearly a contradiction
Since in theology they are equivalent to each other from the prepositions, by and from this they signify neither any division nor difference of the holy Trinity, but the union and immutability, namely according to his nature and will. For from this it is clearly shown that the Father, the Son, and the Holy Spirit are of one and the same nature of power, operation, and will. But he who here took the sayings of the saints and inscribed them, wrongly and impiously tries to show the difference of the divine persons by the equivalence of such prepositions, and that one of the three divine persons, namely the Holy Spirit, has a different essence from the two persons, and from each of them. It is clear, therefore, that the opinions of the saints are good and pious; but from him who thus gathered them together and wrote them down, let them be taken ill and impiously. But the fact that such a preposition, through, signifies union and complete immutability, namely, when these, from, are equivalent, the divine Maximus shows how much more open he is, when he writes to Marinus about some who say that the Spirit is from the Son. He says, in fact, that they did not make the Son the cause, for they knew that the Son and the Holy Spirit had one cause, that is, the Father; but in order to show that they proceed through him, and to prove by this preposition the conjunction of substance and immutability. It is therefore evident from them that Vecchus should

receive such sayings with unbelief and impiety. For he does not try to add from them conjunction and immutability, but the difference of persons, and he does not listen to the great Basil, who in a certain part to Amphilochius, that the Father, [...] says, will create through the Son, does not mean the imperfect creation of the Father, nor the superfluous energy of the Son it shows an operation, but it signifies the union of the will: therefore this word, through the Son, has the confession of the first and principal cause: it is not taken to find an efficient cause. Therefore, what he asserts that the Spirit proceeds through the Son, and from the Son according to a temporal mission, proves very well the same will of the Father and the Son; for by the good will of the Father and the Son, and with the co-operation of the Spirit, the Holy Spirit is given and lavished upon worthy men. But those who follow the Latins, impiously asserting that the holy spirit has its essence through the Son and from the Son, and that it is the work of good pleasure and will, and of necessity a creature, but not a fruit of the divine nature. For the holy Damascene says: The work of the divine will is a creature, but not of the divinity, it is absent. And again, it is not the will, but the generation, as well as the procession, of the divine nature, which is before the ages and eternal. The defense of Nicene. This man is adamant about those authorities which affirm that the Holy Spirit is from the Son and proceeds through the Son from the Father, and that which is gathered from them can in no way be against him. For what is the deal with such a clear truth? But the equivalence of these prepositions, by and from, is neither good nor consistent with any reason, and he pursues his adversary with insults and curses. he is unable to give an account of these, and he purifies this preposition by, even though it signifies the union, immutability, and identity of the will in the holy Trinity, since in theology it is recognized that the preposition is read from the equivalency, it is not possible for anyone according to this meaning to accept it even from the procession of the Holy Spirit from the Father through the Son , or we do not even understand it by that reason, but rather to introduce distinction and division, and opposition and discord. From what has been said he himself seems to understand; nay, he asserts most plainly that by this

DEFENSE OF THE ORTHODOX CATHOLIC DOCTRINES

means we all want to have the essence of the Holy Spirit differently from the two persons of the Father and the Son. Thus he thinks us experts in theology: but perhaps he also feels this, asserting that the world was created from the Father through the Son; for I do not see any necessity why, indeed, of the creature, through, equivalent, it signifies the identity of persons: Lamen showing discretion (for he himself will not deny this), but of the Spirit, diversity and altogether discretion. Nor is he ashamed to bring against himself the testimony of the great Basil: to have that voice through the profession of the Son as the main cause. But we say that we have the existence of two persons, the Father and the Son, the Holy Spirit, and we confess it with all our hearts. For nothing works except in so far as this is something and an individual. But in so far as the Father and the Son are two of that kind: but to proceed differently from them, we by no means grant this. For as the natural operation of the Father, so also of the Son, we hear the saints saying that the Holy Spirit is. But we believe that the operation of the Father and the Son is primarily one, unless he also says that the world subsists when he proceeds from the Father, and the Son, and the Spirit, or from the Father through the Son in the Spirit; He asserted that he was not made of three persons alone; for this he would of course admit, but also differently from the three: that if he marvels in what accord with this preposition, representing the unity and identity of the will, we wish to demonstrate by it that the Son is the cause of the existence of the Holy Spirit: first he marvels at himself, saying how the world was made by the Son, and then him He supposes the cause of the production of the world to be shown by this preposition; or he may say that the Son is not the cause of beings, and evil will run with evil. He also brings the testimony of the divine Maximus, which does not at all serve the purpose. And for we admit that the preposition, by, signifies the unity and immutability of the substance of the Father and the Son: we know, indeed, by this saying, by, a certain order and its respect, of which this is said to him of whom we use this saying, from, especially to be shown; yet the same identity and immutability are the cause, and that the Son can be the same as the Father, and that the Holy Spirit proceeds through him. For according to the divine Cyril from both, from the Father through the Son, but according to the same Great One, who proceeds from the Father and the Son, or from the Father through the Son, that is, he has existence. They give the spirit. But what the holy teacher says, that he does not make the Son the cause of the Holy Spirit, but the Father, you will not be surprised if you consider the Greek language, and of which it is properly accustomed to use this name as the cause. For it is well known that the first and principal cause, and the source, and the root of each one is properly called this cause, such as no one would admit being the Father alone, which is clear from this, since no one who is considered a Christian would deny that there is a cause of creatures and the Holy Spirit. But the theologian Gregory. God, says he, consists in three great things, the cause and the workman, and the finisher, that is, the Father, and the Son, and the Holy Spirit. But when you hear the Father as the main cause, don't think that we already say differently, that the Son produces the Spirit, since it is not the main cause. For the same thing nevertheless also follows from the creature, and simply to all that the Son has, whatever the Father also has: for the Son is not the main cause of the creature, since as causally and as the Son he has all things, whatever the Father has paternally, and not causally. He is the cause, and together with the Father is the cause of beings. And neither their unity nor the unity of the will, nor the distinction of persons, is represented by the preposition. But which, he says, is the work of the divine will, and therefore we call the creature the Spirit because of this expression, through which it represents the identity of the will. I do not know if they can be seen by anyone other than themselves. For if, because it shows the identity of the will, it is inferred that it is a creature of the Spirit, why should it not rather be a divine nature and be thought by us to be present? Why, with the opinion of the blessed Maximus, which he brought for himself, he should rather teach the identity of the substance: for, he says, to show the conjunction of the substance, although and if only the identity of the will were to be shown by it, nothing absurd would follow even thus, since the same thing, and essence, and the will of God is called For there is no one who does not know that this power is

DEFENSE OF THE ORTHODOX CATHOLIC DOCTRINES

simpler and more sublime than all. It is evident to all that each one has the power to do more things, as much as it is simpler and more sublime. Wherefore also the will of God to the Son, and to the Holy Spirit, as nature or essence, but as the will to the creature. For it is very well known that every will, even the divine will, is determined to an end, as nature has it, desiring itself in a determined way, just as nature also has a determined nature to one. nature As for those which are at the end, and above all those without which the end can be reached, as they are of creatures, for these contribute nothing either to the presence of God, or to a better being: to these, I say, do not determine, and therefore as the will is; for it is clear that she both wills and wills. Hence the opinion of Damascene is resolved, and we are freed from all criticism, since those words which seemed to be against us, bring nothing necessary. Therefore, when he seemed to have said something, he concluded completely against himself.

According to Vecchus's argument.
are concerned, which therefore indicate that the Holy Spirit is from the Father through the Son, and these sentences which immediately show that the Son is from the Father have been collected, in order to confirm those sentences which show that the Holy Spirit is through the Son. For if the Holy Spirit were not through the Son, why should he not be said to be directly from the Father?

Palamas contradiction.
The Holy Spirit is also said to be directly from the Father, whence that opinion of yours, and every effort is destroyed. But Nyssenus, together with several others, says that they both belong to the one person of the Father in the same way, apart from the mode of subsistence. But what about those who say that the Holy Spirit proceeds from the Father, and remains in the Son, and that he penetrates from the Father into the Son, and that he is from the Father, and that he is accompanied by the Word? Likewise, those who assert that the communion of charity of the Father and the Son is the Holy Spirit, besides those who regard each person as having no less relation to the other than to himself. What, then, is he

who says: Your hands have made me and fashioned me? Do not all these, then, immediately show that the Holy Spirit is from the Father?

The defense of Nicene.
Nor indeed do we at all deny that the Holy Spirit proceeds directly from the Father, although this was not expressly stated by the teachers. If, therefore, you also confess with us that he is mediately, the matter is for us; and the middle person of the Son between the Father and the Holy Spirit. But from here you are deceived, since you cannot distinguish between which covenant the Spirit is directly from the Father, and which covenant is also mediate. For if we were to admit that the Holy Spirit is from the Father and the Son in two and different processions, so that indeed he proceeds imperfectly from the Father, but perfectly from the Son; Now, however, if anyone looks to the single production and procession of identity from both, and likewise that the Father is both the cause and the source of the divinity, so that if he were not, the Son himself would not be, nor would he be the cause of anyone, he will find the Spirit directly from the Father; and what you yourself say leads to these things. But if everyone looks into the order, who is in fact in the Trinity, and not only in our intention, he will see the Son as the middle, and the Spirit as the third from the Father, and through the Son proceeding from the Father, and having the Son preconceived before him, just as the Son has the Father preconceived. You do not necessarily conclude that you are not thinking at all.

Vecchus' third argument.
These are also the sentences of the Scriptures, which contribute to the mind of the teachers who prove that the Spirit comes from the Father, not directly, but through the Son. For if the Spirit were directly from the Father, it would not be said that the Son is the image of the Father, and the Spirit the image of the Son, the Son is the operation of the Father, and the Spirit is the operation of the Son, the Son is the person of the Father, the Spirit is the person of the Son.

DEFENSE OF THE ORTHODOX CATHOLIC DOCTRINES

Palamas contradiction.
Most of all, you who here describe impious things, which are rightly called by the saints, how do you not see that the common and natural things of the holy Trinity have no difference, since there is one God, one image, one will, and finally one operation of the Father, and of the Son, and of the Holy Spirit Therefore, together with others, even when the second person of the other is said of these, it is natural, and not personal, and indicative of an unchangeable similitude, but it does not show a subsisting mode, it is absent. You, however, do not thus say the other person of another person, but hypostatically understand these things: you cannot henceforth be a preacher of the Trinity. For if the Son is the person of Paris, as from him, the Spirit of the Son, the Father will not be another person besides the Son, nor the Son besides the Holy Spirit. Do you see how the words of the saints are indeed pious and righteous, but from you they are received impiously and perversely?

The defense of Nicene.
Thus, you hear blessed also Paul, who affirms the image of the invisible Son of God, and the splendor of his person, and the splendor of his glory; as if he were to say that he is the same person with the Father, and by nature he would only show the identity, and not also the distinction of persons. But we, who are guided by faith and reason, and understand the identity of nature by these names to be an image, that is to say, to destroy the unity of the holy Trinity and the image of the sound of the operation, so that we can also have the divinity as a model, receiving the image in the same way, and saying the person of the Father, the substance of the Father we show that since in God the substance is the same as his person, we show no less the distinction of persons. For we admit that there are three holy persons in the Trinity, not by this showing identity, but distinction: and the image certainly does not refer to itself, but to that of which it is also an image; and therefore, signifies hypostasis, since it is a relative noun and constitutes a person. As for you, I don't know how you understand that, since it is naturally said not as you assert postically: when the second person is said to be another, and

you think that it is inappropriate to bring something against us, which is clearly against you. For those who say to us that the Son is the person of the Father, proceeding from him, and the Son again the Holy Spirit, as proceeding from him, do you think it follows from this that we do not say that the Father is another person, and the Son another, and the Holy Spirit. But I, if I understand your reason well, would assert that from this position of yours the most absurd thing follows; from ours it is quite the opposite. For if the second person of the other is said to be merely identical, and shows an unchangeable likeness, as you put it: but the person of the Father is the Son, as the same with him in substance, and likewise the Son of the Spirit, as of the same substance only with him, surely you do not give another person of the Father, as The Son and the Holy Spirit, nor theirs from each other. For they are not of another substance, but when we hear the person of the Father or the person of the Son, and also understand the identity of the Holy Spirit with substance; so that, according to you, the Trinity ceases to be limited to a single God. But if, as we say, the second person of another is said to be from him, whose being is also said to be, and at the same time to be of the same substance: since whatever is from something is clearly different, at least substance and person, than that from which it is said to be. How can the Father not be another person, and the Son, and the Holy Spirit? And so we indeed, asserting these things, observe the Trinity as much as possible; you, however, be careful not to do the opposite, and unjustly rebuke us, of whom you yourself are worthy, by bringing insults upon us. Now when a thing is said to be the person, or power, or operation of anyone, it signifies another hypostasis or person to this, it also signifies that it is from him, of which it is said to be. Hear what they all say: Who is the power of God, and the wisdom of God; as well as the living and subsisting operation and power of the Father's Son. And again, the Holy Spirit is not alien from the Son, but in him, and from him, and as a natural operation. For it is clear that since the Son is the subsisting power of the Father, he also differs from him in so far as he is a hypostasis, and according to this he is also from him, and the Holy Spirit is the natural operation of the Son, nor this non-subsisting, and being from him, and

DEFENSE OF THE ORTHODOX CATHOLIC DOCTRINES

in this respect distinguished from him. Wherefore these names show not only the identity of the nature in which you praise yourself, but also the distinction of people. Therefore, having been conquered by reason, all the conflicts which follow are at the same time dispelled.

Vecchus' fourth argument.
When some are inclined to declare that the Son is the middle in the Trinity, which, however, was clearly established by the holy Fathers in theology, they do not at all want to assert the name of order in the Trinity; and these authorities of the teachers have been collected, both to show that the Holy Spirit is connected with the Father through the Son, and also to demonstrate clearly that there is order in the Trinity.

Palamas contradiction.
You lie against pious and faithful men, most pitifully. For we are not ignorant of the existence of order in the Trinity; but pious and faithful. But he who shows that the Holy Spirit is of necessity from the Father, as impious, whom you assert with Eunomius, we do not at all accept. And you lie against the opinions of the Scriptures. They say that not only the Son, but sometimes also the Father is connected with the Son and the Holy Spirit; And the order which you claim to be clearly stated, is manifest, that it is not of the Son and the Holy Spirit. It is granted, however, that the Son is also the medium, but not as regards the existence of the Spirit by those who know the divine, but a secret confession, not directly to those who place the Holy Spirit, lest he also be seen to be begotten. And so the sayings of the holy men were well and rightly preserved. But he who has collected them in this place and added to his own a false opinion, uses them badly and impiously.

The defense of Nicene.
But whoever you are who says these things, such an order as you have brought, and the listeners of your teachings, should not be called order, but rather disorder. For if, for the sake of confession, as you say, you

establish an order, and assert that the Son is the middle, lest by placing the Spirit directly you should be forced to think that he was begotten, you see that you do not really put order into the divine Trinity, but that he himself, by conceiving it, bestows it as a gift, and thinks that it is in you when you will. by changing the order of the names. For if, because of the name of the Father (for I think you call this a confession) you do not immediately bring forth the Holy Spirit, lest it should be thought that He was begotten, although if we call Him breathing, we immediately bring forth the Spirit, and through the Spirit from breathing is the Son, and the Son by himself from the Father, but accidentally from breathing: But the Spirit was sent forth by himself from breathing, but from the Father by accident, and to be in us who alter the order. Sometimes we put the Son as the middle of the Father and the Spirit, when we call the Father the first cause; Indeed, all these things are absurd, and lead to disorder rather than order. But we deny such an order. Nor indeed do you think that we, with Eunomius, feel that we are in order, and that we think the Spirit third by necessity from the Father. For we believe that the third is the most important, and this is out of necessity. But this word to you does not of necessity mean the same thing, and by nature, when we inherit with him who delivered him to be the third in the tradition of saving baptism. Go, he says, and baptize in the name of the Father, and of the Son, and of the Holy Spirit. But we never say that we are fearful by nature, nor do we ever cut into one of the opposites by avoiding the other, as you do yourself. For if you flee from the third nature yourself, you also deny the very discretionary order of persons; nor can you remain in the middle: how much better it would have been for you to flee from both extremes, and to stand in the middle, as is our opinion: which we neither completely deny that there is a third, nor allow the third to exist by nature, but indeed positing him as third, not only to be said, but also to be and Who can deny that the receivers of a discretionary order are persons, not natures, which indeed is of necessity? Although he himself shows that all order in any way is of necessity, do not allow this to be the third, nor listen to our Father Chrysostom when he says: The discrete order of the divine persons, known as the sanctus, consists, but the discrete order of nature is to be rejected in the Holy Trinity: but the discrete order of the persons of nature is indeed not to be, but to be nature, any one of sound mind would grant, and according to this reason to be and to be natural, not according to what he discerns nature, but according to what nature is not by our position. And this is affirmed by the teachers and leaders of the Church, Athanasius and Basilius here delivering the greater statement, Athanasius bringing in the lesser, and both comprising a single syllogism showing that by nature the Holy Spirit is ordered to the Son; for to the Father the Son is by nature a proper cause; and that which is produced from the heather to the fire itself, Basil teaches; But the Spirit has the same nature and order to the Son, which the Son has to the Father, Athanasius commanded in letters, that when he is natural, he does not discern nature in so far as he is. For this is often said, that the mouths of slanderers may be stopped, but because nature is not our position; that it is in fact, and not by our intention, nor in us, as you yourself judge, when we wish to exchange and sometimes to order in this way, and sometimes otherwise, there is no one who will not admit it. If, therefore, you yourself admit such an order, we have not perverted the sentences of the Scriptures; nor will it be seen by anyone who has a mind: but he who collected them did it well and rightly, and these reasons are for us. But if you deny this, he who says that you deny him, speaks the truth, and does not lie, but well wounds you with the collected words of the teachers. Of course, you do these things basely too, when you yourself collect the said authorities for another opinion, and by them you think to reject this insoluble golden chain of order. For the Spirit is said to be the mediator between the Son and the Father as begotten and begotten, although he is neither begotten nor begotten according to Gregory of Nazianzus. Which, when they are superfluous, and are not produced for the purpose, no less against the producer, than against those against whom they are produced, and have a demonstration of criticism and rudeness.

DEFENSE OF THE ORTHODOX CATHOLIC DOCTRINES

Vecchus's fifth argument.
While there are some who hold that the saying of the Gospel, which calls the Holy Spirit the Spirit of truth, they do not grant that it is the same as valid and that it proceeds from the Father himself. Likewise, they assert that it is not equivalent, that is, to proceed from the Father, and to receive the Holy Spirit from the Son. The authorities of the teachers were also collected to show the equivalence of such evangelical sayings.

Palamas contradiction.
The madness of man! For while these words are equivalent, representing the unity or consubstantiality of the divine Spirit, they differ as if they demonstrate the subsistence of the Spirit from both, that is, the Father and the Son. This indeed is known from the same Scriptures. But he who has brought together these sentences is as if deaf to the difference of these sayings.

The defense of Nicene.
In these he does not even present an apparent argument, which he uses only in others, neglecting the truth, or even ignorant of those in whom he happened to find it. In these also, he would not have found it if he had seemed vehemently, but he afflicts the author with insults, as he also does in others: he also puts forward a certain position, to which there is no need to prove anything. For that authority which the Spirit of truth confesses to the Holy Spirit, is equal to that which He sets forth to proceed from the Father, or to receive from the Son, saying to us: To show to them the unity and consubstantiality of the Spirit; yet not to them to differ the procession from the Father and the Son, for according to this: but he does not demonstrate how, but he testifies to the truth of those authorities and sayings, which nevertheless clearly lead to the opposite of what he wants. For that which signifies a certain community and consubstantiality to each other is equivalent, this is very true. Now that they do not show a procession from the Father and the Son and the Holy Spirit, you certainly bring this from yourself, fighting against all truth. For this very thing is the consubstantial cause, that the Spirit is

DEFENSE OF THE ORTHODOX CATHOLIC DOCTRINES

produced from the Son, or from the Father through the Son; as the divine Cyril clearly shows: The Holy Spirit, he says, is more proper to the Father and the Son, and one from the Father through the Son because of the identity of substance, whether of the Father and the Son, or of both of these to the Spirit. For in one way or another they do these things for us. For the consubstantiality of the Spirit with the Father and the Son, and the fact that they are said to be nearer, does not exclude his being from the Son, or from the Father through the Son; On the contrary, he concludes and proves that he also says the same thing elsewhere: that the Holy Spirit is of God the Father also and of the Son, who proceeds consubstantially from both, that is, from the Father through the Son. For if simply consubstantiality alone were the reason why the Holy Spirit was said to be proper to the Son, certainly the Son would also be said to be proper to the Holy Spirit, since he is consubstantial with him, which no one has ever dared to affirm. If, however, because the Son is related to the Father, he says, it cannot be called the Son proper to the Spirit, lest the Holy Spirit be seen to be his Father: they testify to us that the Son necessarily breathes or produces, for the reason that Spirit, being a relative noun, is related to the breathing It is non-existence, and something is breathed out of it, of which it is also said to be. And so they will be found boasting against themselves, when they think they are attacking their adversaries. That Dautem is not only said to be the proper Spirit of the Son falls into the same sense, and to proceed from the Father, but nevertheless also to receive from the Son, Cyril himself testifies to this again, together with many other teachers, what he has, is said to accept perfectly what is his.

Vecchus' sixth argument.
When there are some who affirm that these words differ from each other, that is, to proceed, to flow forth, and to proceed, they were gathered together for an irrefutable demonstration of their equivalence in view of the opinion of St. Cyril; and that the Holy Spirit should flow forth in those places, to which he will speak, when he proceeds from the Father.

DEFENSE OF THE ORTHODOX CATHOLIC DOCTRINES

Contradiction of Palama.
O madness! For whom is so ignorant as not to know that this word is also said to proceed from the Son, but never to proceed or flow from him himself? Just as it is said to flow properly of the temporal mission of the Spirit, sometimes it is also said of the procession. Yet this old man, and those who follow him, assert that these differ nothing from one another, impudently and impudently alike. Indeed, the sayings of the saints collected in this place, although they show in which these words sometimes coincide, do not in the least destroy the difference of their diction to each other.

The defense of Nicene.
But if you had read the blessed Cyril carefully, you would also have found that he used this expression about the Son in the treatise he made on John, namely in that part, when the Paraclete came. For if, he says, it does not proceed from the Father, that is, from his substance, the Son, according to us, but if it is not said to flow from the Son, yet when it is said of the Spirit, it is not at all surprising; when this expression is adapted to the figure of the name of the Spirit, not before the Son; just as the word generation is indeed adapted to the name of the Son, but not to the name of the Spirit; However, no one would justly say that since it signifies that he is begotten from a cause, but the Spirit is not begotten from the Father, but proceeds, it does not mean that he himself proceeds as from a cause from that from whom he proceeds. For this is a foolish thing to say. Wherefore you cannot at all prove the difference between these sayings. Now when these things are said of the Son and of the Holy Spirit alike: likewise, when the emanation of the Spirit and the procession are called, and the flow and progress as if they all signified the same thing, these names do not seem to differ at all from one another. If they do not differ, then they are to be heard in the same way, when the Holy Spirit is said to proceed with the Son, or through the Son, as with the Father: but when they are said of the Father, we understand by them the procession of the Holy Spirit from him; therefore, the same is also

from the Son, that is, it is to be understood through the Son. For the Holy Spirit flows, as Cyril admits, from the Son; as also from God and the Father, leaving no trace of doubt. But if you show that these names either do not mean the same thing, or if the same thing must be understood differently from the Son and from the Father, although our teacher cries out, that it should flow from the Son, as it is understood from God himself and from the Father: we will absolve you of the guilt of unjust blasphemy in You accuse him of old age and madness, of which you do not consider him rightly.

Vecchus's seventh argument.
When some, hearing that the Holy Spirit emanates and proceeds from the Son, do not insipidly grant the divine nature of the Spirit to arise from the divine substance, and the nature of the Son to arise and emanate: but a certain spiritual gift coming to those who are worthy, and for that reason that indwelling takes place in them with the divinity of the Holy Spirit present everywhere, it is customary to understand such a function as if it were to be understood as separate and separate from the divine substance of the Spirit. Those authorities have been collected from which this can be understood. The indwelling of the Holy Spirit, which happens to the faithful and worthy, although it is habitually ineffable and above reason: nevertheless, because these gifts of the Spirit flow through him, where his divine nature will habitually dwell, the Holy Spirit himself, who is in the Trinity and in one person, and his complement, and who is divine The nature and perfection of God is as the Father and the Son are shown; when someone says that the Holy Spirit emanates, proceeds, and is from the Son.

Palamas contradiction.
He who composed this writing certainly does not know what to say, nor what he wants to affirm. For no one who devoutly understands what has been said, that every divine grace is from divine nature. he would think the operation. And not for that reason, because the divine operation is inseparable from the divine nature, therefore nature is also an operation

that differs nothing from it. Indeed, the divine operation is from nature, and exists in it, as the theologians affirm, but it is not in itself. Indeed, the divine nature is neither from operation, and exists by itself, and is the place of divine operations, but we also affirm that the Holy Spirit is by no means from the person of the Son. But when he says that he is from the nature of the Son, he thinks that he contradicts us and is an adversary: nothing differs, as he seems to think that nature is from subsistence, or even foolishly bringing a difference of nature into the holy Trinity, because there is a difference of persons.

The defense of Nicene.
If, then, you do not think of the divine grace of the Spirit as separate, or of his nature and person, what do you understand when you hear that the Holy Spirit is sent from the Son? that is, that which is sent by the divine nature, and that which is subsisting, which is complementary to the Trinity, that is to say, the person of the Holy Spirit. By what means, then, do you mean to send this Son? For there is nothing other than the Father: for it would also be of another's power; It is clear, then, that just as the Father But the Father sends forth the person himself; therefore the Son sends him himself, producing the person himself, unless you call him as a minister to send the Spirit who proceeds from the Father afterwards. Which is as absurd as it is impious. For it is granted that the divine operation is not the same as the divine substance; What do you then try to conclude from this? If when the Holy Spirit is sent, I do not send non-existent grace, but the divine subsisting nature itself, and you yourself allow it. from the Father, which he proposed to be shown to him, who collected the opinions of the doctors. But if you wonder, by what agreement do we, asserting that the Holy Spirit originates from the nature of the Son, and emanates from him, and that he is from his person, as if we were to posit the identity of nature and persons, or because of their difference, we would also introduce the otherness of nature. Indeed, we are much more surprised at your treachery. If, when you hear the nature of the Son with this addition of the Son, you understand it as something simply absolute, and not with the property

DEFENSE OF THE ORTHODOX CATHOLIC DOCTRINES

of the Son, and you could not even comprehend that by itself nature, taken absolutely and collectively, can neither send nor produce anything, nor be at all the cause of being, which it should not be taken with any property that constitutes a person. For the whole philosophy cries out that they are the activities of individuals.

Vecchus' eighth argument.
In order to demonstrate that the Holy Spirit is from the Father and the Son, there are also the authorities of the Scriptures, which show that he is a quality of the substance of the Father and the Son. Also, fragrance, breath, and smell; and next to such sentences, other sayings have been extracted: which lead to the same sense, which both the Father, the source of the Holy Spirit, and the Son, the source of the Holy Spirit, most piously asserted.

Contradiction of Palamas.
The opinions of the writers here collected by certain examples show, as far as is possible, that the Holy Spirit is consubstantial with the Father and the Son. For no one can find an example that lacks any kind of likeness. And when the Holy Spirit is sometimes called living water according to grace and operation, the source of this water is called both the Father and the Son. Sometimes the Holy Spirit is the same. But he who brought such sayings here, passed over some of them, was abused by some. And in this way, he thinks to attract and draw his listeners to his perverted senses.

The defense of Nicene.
Indeed, the aforesaid sentences demonstrate the consubstantiality of the Holy Spirit with the Father and the Son, and not only that, but also that he is and proceeds from them. For of course it is from the Father, and you yourself allow it to be signified. But when you grant this, you will not be able to give an account why the same things said of the Father show not only consubstantiality, but also that they are from him: but of the Son only consubstantiality, especially since these names are not

changed. Indeed, the Son is said to be consubstantial with the Spirit; but the form, or the fragrance, or the breath of it, is never said. Therefore, when we read the Son as the form of the Father, or the fragrance, or the quality, we do not only understand this consubstantial one with him, but we also think that the breath, form, fragrance, and operation of the Son, proceeding from him, and thus the Holy Spirit, are said to be said in both ways aforesaid. For what reason is there to understand these things differently from the Father to the Son and the Spirit, and differently from the Son to the Spirit? You, however, have forgotten what you confessed before. Again, you affirm that the Holy Spirit is only called living water according to grace, and that the Son alone is the source of this. But if this grace is not in the least separated from substance and existence, for you have already granted this), how can the divine person of the Holy Spirit not also be sent forth by the Son as a source with this grace?

Vecchus' ninth argument.
These sentences of the Scriptures, in which the Fathers, professors of sacred theology, demonstrated that all that is proper to the Father naturally passes into the Son and is begotten from him, are collected here to demonstrate that the Holy Spirit proceeds and proceeds from the Son just as much as from the Father: as God Cyril sent letters. For if the determinations of the said sentences take away only paternity and generation from the Son, it is clear that the Son will not be the Father, but the Spirit emanating from the paternal substance, and from the non-begetting substance of the Son both emanates and flows. Contradiction of Palama. Indeed, impiety is strengthened by no reason; For this Vecchus, hearing that the paternal properties pass into the Son, and naturally and essentially of those proper, which are of the paternal substance, thought the teachers to say, not of those which are proper by nature. Therefore, according to his expertise in theology, the divine Cyril writing in his Thesauri, how can God not be a Spirit, since he has all the substantial properties of the Father and the Son? He will have the

personalities of the Father and the Son of the Spirit, and begotten and begotten will be the Father of lights and having the power to beget and produce. In this respect, what can be said to be more impious or more unnecessary? Again, she will understand almost the same thing when she heard Damascene say in one of his Dogmas: Whatever the Father and the Holy Spirit have, except that they are not begotten. And Gregory of Nazianzus, in that discourse which he writes to those who came from Egypt: Whatever there are sons, there are also spirits, besides sonship. How much madness must one think again, when he hears that he is from the substance of the Son, to think that he is also from his person? And if, just as there is one substance, so also subsistence is from God. Furthermore, he does not see that when the Spirit is said to be of the Father and from the Father, those who deny that the Father is the Son equally deny the Sons' communion with the Father according to the progressive property.

The defense of Nicene.
You do not think that this wise man is so ignorant of theology, that he thinks that what belongs to the substance of the father must pass into the Son. Now that the Father produces the Holy Spirit, not in so far as the Father has, but in so far as he breathes. Now this noun spirator is by no means a constitutive noun of a person. For this reason, it is not impossible that this also is common to the Son; if we are to believe the most holy Father Cyril, who knows much better about theology than we do. He says that the Son is all that the Father is, except that which alone is not the Father. Then he adds, having his own from him, and in him in nature the Holy Spirit. Nor did these adversaries among themselves think that the Son is not the Father, and yet that the Spirit is from him. Of course, it has been decided that it is one thing in so far as he is the Father, and another in so far as he is the breather, and that this is indeed incommunicable to the Son, but this must agree as much as possible. And explaining this elsewhere more clearly, he says, not only that he is not the Father, but also that he does not beget. Evidently, paternity only and only the power of procreation, not taking away from him the power

of breathing. But whether you are trying to deceive us or yourself, I do not know by what the divine Cyril said. And even if it seems to have something in common with the things proposed, yet we shall find that they differ greatly, if we look carefully. For what difference does it make to say that anyone has the natural property of another, or whose properties are natural? For that refers only to identity in substance: this signifies the community of certain personal ideas, which is naturally and substantially, so that no room is given to any accident or participation. And that, namely, all things that are of the Father, and that the Spirit is besides being begotten; and whatever sons are also Spirits besides sonship, I do not know whose grace he added. For we happily and piously understand all these things. But if anyone himself does not feel well, or tries to deceive others, it is his crime. For if anyone takes away from the Spirit the property of the Father, which is to be begotten, and the cause or principle of other persons, what further personal property of the Father will they leave to him? Similarly, if someone, comparing the Son to the Spirit and these alone to each other, denied that the Spirit is the Son, but believed that in other respects he was completely similar to the Son, how would he attribute personal property to him? Nor would he give his father's name. For the conversation was not about the Father, nor was that comparison to him, nor, although it had been to him, would he have left anything of the Father's property to him. Since, apart from the fact that he is not the Son, all other things are according to the Son, and at all, just as the Son is thus himself caused by the Father, but not filial to whom? For that is personal to the Son, to be the Son. Which we have already received from the Spirit; But as to the fact that if anyone hears the Spirit of the Son from his substance, he also understands him from his person, it is not to be wondered at, it has been sufficiently said before. And here it is a great folly, he says, not to consider that when it is said of the Father and of the Spirit from the Father, those who deny that the Son is the Father, at the same time deny that the power of breathing is common to the Son and the Father. Accusing himself, perhaps, of the same insanity, perhaps a greater one, while he understands this absurdity, nevertheless does not escape it, when he calls the Spirit the Spirit of the

DEFENSE OF THE ORTHODOX CATHOLIC DOCTRINES

Son. For if of the Father, and from the Father, as he admits, it is called the Spirit: those who deny that the Son is the Father, deny not only that the power of breathing is common to the Son with the Father, but also that they are called the Spirit of the Son. But if he escapes well from this madness, he falls into another, much more detestable, namely, if he does not speak of the Holy Spirit, and does not feel the Spirit of the Son; which, in short, who would not say to every adversary of the Scriptures? And so, this speech is also evidently found to be full of ignorance on every side.

Vecchus' tenth argument.
O the sentences of the Scriptures, in which the Fathers, treating of divinity, affirmed that the Son is the proper Son of the Father, that he exists from his essence, and that he is from him as the proper of his substance, have been collected here, so that everyone who wills may have the opportunity to know clearly from this; , which is from its substance. And for the same reason it is said to be from the substance of the Son, because good is proper to such a substance. This also shows the consubstantiality of the Spirit with the Son. For if according to some other reason of consubstantiality, such as that which is said of two consubstantialities; in which there is not one for the other, the Spirit would be proper to the Son, and the substance would be from the Son; he would feel with faith. But such consubstantiality is not properly consubstantiality; but that which joins the one to the other, as if through him existing naturally and substantially from him. This will be proved by the opinion here cited of the great Basil, who plainly asserts that brothers are not properly said to be consubstantial with one another. And to such propositions are added other propositions, which for this reason show that the Son is consubstantial with the Father, because he is of his substance, so that all who wish may understand from this, therefore, that the Holy Spirit is consubstantial with the Son, because he is of his substance. Also, to strengthen these sentences, other sayings of the

Fathers are brought forward, which show the consubstantiality of the Spirit with the Father and the Son from thence, that it is from the Father through the Son.

Palamas contradiction.
The Son is more properly the Son of the Father, as begotten of him, and in the same way is the Holy Spirit, as proceeding from the Father. Just as the great Basil commanded in a letter against the Eunomians: I know the propriety, he says, of the Holy Spirit to the Father, because he proceeds from the Father. He is said, however, to be the Son of the Spirit, as the same passage asserts in the eighth chapter to Amphilochius, as being conjoined to him according to nature; for it is absolutely impossible that those things which are the same in nature should not be conjoined with each other. But it is not called the Son of the Holy Spirit, lest the Holy Spirit should be seen to be the Father, when the Son is referred to the Father, whose Son he would be called. But this old man gathers nothing sound from the opinions here collected; He is, however, criticized by himself, when he says that because of the consubstantiality of the substance of the Son, the Spirit is said to be. For it was not for that reason even from the person of the Son; for it will happen that these things come from one another. Therefore no one has ever asserted that the Spirit is from the person of the Son, but from the person of the Father.

The defense of Nicene.
It is not only enough to say, but we must also add reason. What a voluntary position is this, to call the Father's own Son, or the Holy Spirit, as having an essence from the Father: but saying the Son's own Spirit is not to be understood in the same way, that he has essence from the Son, but whom he imagines at will, as if in dreams. For what was said by the great Basil in the midst of the leader, you brought rather for us, and against yourself. Indeed, of one and the same thing, namely, that the Holy Spirit is naturally conjoined to the Father and the Son, the most

holy teacher, seeking proofs, brings this as the most important, namely, that it proceeds from the Father, and is called the Son, and is, and brings it into the middle, thinking that they refer to the same thing, and that both these things are the same. For he whose Spirit is said to be, in short, is breathed from him. But you see the absurdity of the matter, and his following positions, and the necessary conversion, which it follows from your words when you try to escape, even unwillingly favoring your adversaries. For it is not said (say) Son of the Holy Spirit: lest the Son of this Father should be seen, asserting, of course, that he and he should be relative to one another, so that with the Spirit the name is relative: just as he himself willingly and unwillingly admits that he is related to the one who breathes, and is breathed from him! He must, of whom it is called the Spirit. But even if the Holy Spirit is said to be from the substance of the Son, it is not therefore thought necessary that it should also be from his person, something also absurd. I really don't know what you are trying to point out. For in this way you say that they were from each other, as if it were possible that the Son should also be said to be substance from the Spirit; and therefore, also from his person. If I perceive you well, for you yourself say nothing clear; and our reason is thereby most firmly strengthened; for you will never find either the Son or the Father, neither in the Sacred Letters, nor among the teachers, that it was said from the substance of the Holy Spirit. But if this expression, namely, the substance of the Son or of the Father, signified only consubstantiality, as you wish, it should also be said to be perfect. If before no one of the saints had preached that the Spirit was from the person of the Son, yet they affirmed that he was from the Son, and that he existed from the Son, which above all signifies the existence of the Spirit. But the Western Fathers and teachers also asserted that he proceeded from the Son. But by the name of the Son, unless you understand the person of the Son, it would be a miracle that you should not have said that the Spirit is from the person of the Father, except to Grego alone. Rius Nyssenus, and indeed once in his discourses, had said that the Spirit proceeds from the paternal person, but when you hear from the Father (which sentence is full of all Scripture), you understand everything rather than the person of the Father. But this is most childish. Which of you, therefore, should conclude nothing sane, then, or Vecchus, as our speech has clearly shown.

Vecchus' eleventh argument.
When some, hearing that the Holy Spirit is from the substance of the Son, say that it is one thing from the substance, another from the person; nor can they understand that this name Son is a personal name, and he who says from the substance of the Son shows the whole Son as substance, that is, subsisting. Therefore, to rebuke their senseless and absurd sensibilities, there are also the sentences of the Scriptures, which show that the Son is begotten from the substance of the Father. For if we admit that the birth of the Son from the Father is one, by what agreement can they differ, that is, being from substance, and being from person? Unless anyone should openly blaspheme, and dare to say, that there is one birth of the Son from the substance of the Father, and another from the person. There are also added to these sentences other sayings of the Fathers, which show the perfect substance, and God the Father perfect, and the Son perfect substance, and the Holy Spirit perfect substance.

Contradiction of Palama.
When something is of one substance and one person, then what naturally has essence from that substance also has the same essence from that person, and vice versa. For what existed from that person is also from that substance. But what is of several persons is from that one substance, not from all the other persons, but from one of them. Therefore, since the supreme and most venerable Trinity is one nature in three persons, not everything that has its existence from the others, even from all the persons, but from one of them, that is, the first. For it cannot possibly be from this. Therefore, not from another, but from this one, indeed from one. This is evident in men. For each one of us is indeed Adam from subsistence, but not from his person, since he is one

substance of men, but of many persons from the beginning, since he is human substance, and the person, that is, Hades was one, and Eve was his substance, also formed from his person it is. And before there was Cain, when there was only one manly substance and person, Cain was born from that one manly substance and person of Hades. Now with the two men already existing in the second person, Enoch was indeed from the substance of Hades, but he was not from the person, but was born of Cain only in the person. But this Vecchus, asserting in this place that the Spirit is from the person of the Son, because it is said by the theologians to be from his substance, he posits that there is one person in God as a substance, or he miserably denies the Father altogether. Likewise, he shows that the Holy Spirit is the essence of the Son alone. And from the sayings of those who affirm that in the divine the Father is of perfect substance, and the Son of perfect substance, and likewise the Holy Spirit, he does not understand the unity of substance and the immutability of the three persons, but foolishly tries to speculate on a certain multiplicity and difference in the same Trinity.

The defense of Nicene.
What similar and beautiful examples do you introduce in theology? That is certainly the cause of your error. You are just as wise about the divine as you are about the human, and from here you draw the whole similitude to it. But be careful not to feel this way about that ineffable Trinity. For as the unity of the divinity is to him, so the Trinity of persons must be preserved, lest you be forced to assert that there are three gods, as you manifestly do with these words. For not as three persons have their substance common to each other, so also the divine essence of the persons of the Holy Trinity. Indeed, humanity is the same for them, not in number. But the Holy Trinity has the same number as the divine essence, or divinity, and therefore there are three persons and one essence, and one God. And this indeed subsists in three divine persons, and with each of them there is one subsisting. Humanity, however, does not subsist in particular men, nor is it one subsisting with individual individuals. Wherefore what is of their substance is by no

means also of the person of all. For Cain, since his substance and nature are from Hades and Abel, his person is indeed also from Hades; not because it was from his substance, but because it is from his person, having him himself as the cause. But although the substance is from Abel, it is not from his person, because the person of Abel does not share substance with Hades, not in number, but only in kind. It has neither subsisted in itself as its own substance, nor one subsisting with the second person. But the fact that the substance is from the Father and the Son, nothing prevents it from being from their person also. Nay, indeed, it is absolutely necessary that it should be, since from its substance it is the same and common to the Father and the Son, not merely according to that example of men, and also subsists in these divine persons, that is to say, paternity and sonship. And so the Holy Spirit would also be from his own substance and person, if he did not attack his property: with the same number, that substance is also predicated of him, and he similarly subsists in him. I do not know what they mean by the different examples, or what he can conclude from them. It is true that this is the custom of the contentious, that they oppose themselves even to the manifest, and close their ears to the truth, and do not understand that they will go even to great precipices, so long as they can do anything against those whom they think are their adversaries. Such is the present discourse. He evidently falls into the heresy of those who think there are three gods. Here, however, he tries to impose his God on others as imprudently as possible: and even those who before opposed the Holy Spirit, when they heard that it was from the Father or the Son, accepted that it was indeed from their person, but denied that it was from their substance. But now they are waging a second, more terrible war. For they receive that he is from their substance, but not at all from their person. Thus the holy enemy of the Church never ceases to spread scandals. It is indeed necessary that they should come, but woe to that man through whom they come. Although perhaps some forgiveness should be given to them, indeed they would have to bring some trace of forgiveness with something in their testimony, which was from the divine persons, but not from the substance, which is clear about creatures. But what excuse

DEFENSE OF THE ORTHODOX CATHOLIC DOCTRINES

will there be for these, when they admit that he is from his substance, but from his person, from whose substance they admit that he is, they deny. Thus, they say to themselves and to those who fight against the truth.

The twelfth argument of Vecchus.
When some dare to say that the Holy Spirit emanates from the Son, comes forth, shines forth, and is manifested, they do not mean that he is substantially and personally from the Son, but a certain distribution of spiritual graces from him. They show from the Father. For no one would ever say that the Son does not emanate, does not shine, and does not manifest substantially from the Father, but his graces or gifts.

Palamas contradiction.
That which has its essence from something, either by generation or procession, is also said to proceed from it, and be emitted, and shine forth, and the like. and it is in its own subsistence. But he who collected these authorities, shameless and rash as he is, accuses them of rashness, who have a pious and right understanding of the divine.

The defense of Nicene.
Bring also the necessity, by which all names are equivalent to this, namely, to be generated, to proceed, to come forth, to emanate, to arise, and the like. As for the production of the Spirit from the Son, they are not the same as proceeding from the rest of the same kind. Or what is the reason why what goes forth also emanates, and not the other way around? Not so simply, and without reason, as if asking the audience to admit whatever you want out of grace. But if you think that he himself, speaking these things without demonstration, has done something vigorous, we will also simply contradict you in the same way; and perhaps faith will be used so much more for us, the better and truer we speak to ourselves. For indeed this may perhaps be found of creatures: namely, that which is sent, or emanates, or emanates, or arises from something, does not even have its essence from that, in which it is one thing to be, and another to be sent: although not of them universally,

nor of all these names can be clearly said. For when something arises or emanates from a certain thing, it is necessary that it also be from that thing. But concerning the Holy Trinity, what is the reason why that which desires to be from something should arise and emanate from it, but that which arises and emanates must not also be from it, especially since these names are in it, that is to say, arise, come forth and proceed, as well as sent, signify the same thing, even if they sometimes differ in reason. Wherefore it is plainly evident that even this speech is neither well spoken, nor does it bring anything necessary, nor, in short, anything of truth. He who is like his superiors, bears witness to a similar weakness and error to himself and to them.

The Scriptorium Project is the work of a small group of lay people of various apostolic churches who are interested in the preservation, transmission, and translation of the works of the early and medieval church. Our efforts are to make the works of the church fathers accessible to anyone who might have an interest in Christian antiquities and the theological, philosophical, and moral writings that have become the bedrock of Western Civilization.

To-date, our releases have pulled from the Greek, Syriac, Georgian, Latin, Celtic, Ethiopian, and Coptic traditions of Christianity, and have been pulled from sundry local traditions and languages.

Other Selections from the Byzantine Church Series:

Funeral Oration for Bessarion by Michael Apostolius (Mar. 2007)
Treatise on Sobriety by Nicephorus the Solitary (Apr. 2007)
Defense of the orthodox Catholic Doctrines of the Latins by John Bessarion (Mar. 2009)
Sermons by Nestorius of Constantinople (May 2009)
Theophrastus by Aeneas of Gaza (Apr. 2011)
Treatise on Prayer by St. Evargius of Ponticus (May 2011)
The Lausiac History by St. Palladius of Galatia (Mar. 2013)
Letter on the Fall of Constantinople by Isidore of Kiev (Oct. 2013)
The Hesychast by Gregory of Sinai (June 2015)
Selected Laws by Justinian I, Emperor of Rome (July 2018)
Exhortation to Monks Ordained in India by St. John of Karpathos (March 2021)
Fragments of 'Chronicle' by Hippolytus of Thebes (May 2023)
The Life of the Blessed Theotokos by Epiphanius Monachus (July 2023)
Letters of Nestorius by Nestorius of Constantinople (Sept. 2023)

www.ingramcontent.com/pod-product-compliance
Lightning Source LLC
LaVergne TN
LVHW051922060526
838201LV00060B/4140